IMAGES
of America

BEALE AIR FORCE BASE DURING THE COLD WAR

The workhorses of Strategic Air Command (SAC) at Beale Air Force Base (AFB) are shown on display during the Cold War. From left to right are a KC-135 Stratotanker, a SR-71 Blackbird, and a B-52 Stratofortress carrying two AGM-28 Hound Dog nuclear cruise missiles on its inner wing pylons.

ON THE COVER: KC-135A aircrew members of the 4126th Strategic Wing at Beale AFB scramble to their aircraft. The KC-135 tankers were the quickest to start up and get airborne and were usually parked the closest to the alert facility shown in the background.

IMAGES
of America

BEALE AIR FORCE BASE DURING THE COLD WAR

James B. Quest

ARCADIA
PUBLISHING

Published by Arcadia Publishing
Charleston, South Carolina

Printed in the United States of America

Library of Congress Control Number: 2013938650

For all general information, please contact Arcadia Publishing:
Telephone 843-853-2070
Fax 843-853-0044
E-mail sales@arcadiapublishing.com
For customer service and orders:
Toll-Free 1-888-313-2665

Visit us on the Internet at www.arcadiapublishing.com

Chris,
This is all your fault.
— James

CONTENTS

ACKNOWLEDGMENTS

This is about a time in the history of Beale Air Force Base (AFB) that is not well known to many of the airmen serving at the base today. No other era dominated the base's history more than the four decades in which units of the Strategic Air Command's (SAC) nuclear and reconnaissance forces stood alert during the Cold War. The significance of that era is becoming lost as time distances itself from the events. The images of this book serve as a small reminder of those missions, the people, and the sacrifices.

When I was approached by Arcadia Publishing to do this book on Beale AFB, I was already involved in a six-year research project documenting another significant era in the history of the installation. It was through that research that I became aware of the images that were in the files of the 9th Reconnaissance Wing History Office (9 RW/HO). This project would not have been possible without the support from two of the 9 RW/HO historians: Chris Mayse (2006–2010) and Richard Rodrigues (2011–present). Not only have these two gentlemen been good friends over the years, but they have also allowed me access to the historical files that enabled this project to be accomplished.

The technical advisors for this project were Cold War veterans who served as aircrew members and maintainers on the B-52, KC-135, SR-71, and U-2 aircraft mentioned in this book. Almost all were veterans of SAC.

All photographs used in this book are property of the United States Air Force (USAF) and are courtesy of the 9 RW/HO. They have been compiled over the years by unit historians, USAF photographers, and from private collections donated by veterans. The photographers' work, whether official or private, has helped preserve the history of Beale AFB. Most of the names have been lost with time, but wherever possible, those few who have been identified are recognized.

INTRODUCTION

The War Department announced on July 16, 1941, that a great cantonment was to be built near the Northern Californian cities of Marysville and Yuba City. The announcement stated it would be one of 14 great cantonments the War Department planned to build in the United States as part of the National Defense Program, which sought to expand the US Army to 2.8 million men. It was expected to be the home and training facility for 30,000 to 35,000 men and cover an estimated area of 86,000 acres. Warren N. Shingles, president of the Marysville Chamber of Commerce, was the man most responsible for getting the cantonment. He worked tirelessly behind the scenes to acquire all the information needed to attract the War Department's interest to the area. Capt. Franklin W. Fish, construction quartermaster, was given the responsibility for overseeing the design and construction of the great cantonment that was to be built on the site of the township of Erle. It took less than four months to design the installation and nine months to build it. The War Department announced on April 2, 1942, that the name of this cantonment would be Camp Beale, in honor of Brig. Gen. Edward Fitzgerald Beale. Col. A.D. Cowley, the first post commander, signed Order No. 1 on June 27, 1942, making Camp Beale operational, though the bulk of construction was not completed until November 1942. Camp Beale was the largest cantonment built in the western United States during World War II and was the only one specifically built for an armored division—the 13th Armored Division. The camp consisted of four cantonments, which were officially named on March 20, 1943, as the North Cantonment, the West Cantonment, the Central Cantonment, and the East Cantonment. The East Cantonment (present-day Main Base) was built directly on the site of the township of Erle and incorporated its streets into the design. In addition to the cantonments, there were two main facilities—the sewage treatment facility and the ammunition storage facility—and numerous training ranges. The construction culminated in a total of 1,681 structures built within the four cantonments by December 1943.

The first two aircraft assigned to Camp Beale were the L-4B Piper Cubs acquired from the Headquarters, II Armored Corps, and assigned to the 181st Field Artillery Group. T/3 Rudy Niemuyer, chief mechanic, and S/Sgt. Jerome B. Feldt were in charge of assembling the first aircraft. They were assisted by Sgt. Albert Willis, T/5 Leonard Gordon, and Pfc. Euless Ray. Lt. Paul J. Keating, chief pilot, and T/Sgt. Harold Hillman, pilot, also helped the mechanics with the assembly. The maiden flight was launched on May 17, 1943, from the combination baseball diamond, parade ground, and hayfield behind the 181st Field Artillery Group headquarters with Lieutenant Keating at the controls and Technical Sergeant Hillman riding in the observer's seat, where the radio had yet to be installed. A triangular grass airfield was soon built between C Street and D Street along the north side of Sixth Street (present-day Gavin Mandery Drive) and was dubbed the Camp Beale Airport. This was the first flight line established at the installation. Airstrip No. 1 was built next for the 13th Armored Division's aircraft. It was built on the meadows that bordered the east side of the olive groves running along A Street between Sixth Street to the south and Fourteenth Street to the north.

The first Class A Mishap occurred on June 10, 1943, at 0830 hours. A formation of three P-39s from Orville Army Air Field commenced a mock strafing attack on an armor column traveling east on Sixth Street near the intersection of A Street. The P-39s formed up in a single file and swooped in low over the road and commenced a head-on attack. They pulled up sharply and circled around for a second attack upon reaching the end of the column. The first two P-39s went under the power and telephone lines crossing Sixth Street near the intersection of B Street. The third P-39 followed and clipped a telephone pole with its wing tip. It slammed into a depression in the ground approximately 500 yards from the telephone pole. The force of the impact caused the aircraft to bounce up in a somersault and explode into pieces. The fiery wreckage crashed on the side of a hill slightly east of the A Street and Sixth Street intersection. Soldiers from the nearby motor pools rushed to the scene, but it was too late. 2nd Lt. Eugene A. Seagrean, 22, of Los Angeles, California, would be the first airman to die at Camp Beale in the service of his country. He would not be the last.

Camp Beale was declared surplus at the end of World War II. All the buildings were supposed to have been sold off and the former landowners given "first refusal" rights to the land. Most of the buildings had been sold off by 1948 when the newly formed United States Air Force (USAF) laid claim to the camp and its lands in order to build the Beale Bomb and Gunnery Range in support of the Radar Navigator Bomb School, based at Mather AFB near Sacramento, California. This claim to the land and the planned dropping of bombs on it resulted in a huge backlash of protest from most of the local citizens; the local communities became hostile towards the Air Force.

Maj. Lassiter Thompson would become the first USAF officer assigned to Camp Beale. He arrived on June 24, 1948, with 32 enlisted airmen from Mather AFB to start setting up a "permanent installation." Major Thompson made a personal appeal to the local citizens out of concern for the safety of his men: "We hope the civilians realize the boys stationed here have nothing to do with the making of policy in Washington. We wouldn't want them to have to bear the burden of any feeling against the bombing range." The first bombs were dropped on Camp Beale on the morning of August 9, 1948, by four B-25J bombers from Mather AFB.

The Beale Bomb and Gunnery Range was transferred from the Air Training Command (ATC) to the Continental Air Command (CONAC) on April 29, 1951, in the preparation for building a more permanent installation. Engineers were already on-site, building new facilities and improving on the infrastructure. The installation was renamed Beale Air Force Base on November 27, 1951, by General Order 77 of the Department of the Air Force. This quiet rural part of Northern California was about to become part of the United States' front line during the Cold War.

One

SCARWAF

The new Air Force faced several challenges in its first few years. Among them was the need for an engineering force to support its operations. The Army's aviation engineer forces that had built the airfields during the Allied advances during World War II were reactivated in the 1950s to meet the needs of the Korean War and to train an engineer force for the Air Force, the forerunners of today's Red Horse units. The aviation engineer forces that ended up with the Air Force were designated as Special Category Army Reassigned With the Air Force (SCARWAF) and conducted training at three main locations—Beale AFB, California; Patrick AFB, Florida; and Wolters AFB, Texas.

The 2275th Air Base Squadron was activated at Beale AFB on April 9, 1951, to oversee the SCARWAF units assigned to the base. The first SCARWAF units to arrive were assigned to the 136th Engineer Aviation Brigade (136 EAB) with follow-on brigades and battalions rotating regularly. SCARWAF had a dual mission of training engineers and improving the installation's infrastructure. A large tent city of engineer aviation battalions grew up over the next few months. Training encompassed skills in carpentry, plumbing, electrical, the use of heavy equipment, and so forth. The engineers were then assigned projects such as improving roads, bridges, sewage, and drainage ditches. They built dormitories, motor pools, offices, storage facilities, and ranges. The Explosive Ordnance Disposal (EOD) units cleaned up the bomb ranges.

A popular myth about the three bridges on Gavin Mandery Drive, near base housing, is that they were built to represent the narrow European bridges the armor forces training at Camp Beale were expected to encounter during World War II. The truth is the original three bridges were built in the 1920s and were one-lane wide. The 832nd Engineer Aviation Battalion widened the bridges to two lanes and added a fourth bridge as part of Project 301-53-D between October 18, 1954, and April 1, 1955.

The SCARWAF mission ended on March 1, 1956. The engineers left behind the foundation of a vastly improved installation ready to meet the challenges of a new mission.

B-25J S/N: 44-30742 of the new United States Air Force (USAF) is seen on the tarmac of the Alicia Airport (present-day Yuba County Airport) near Marysville, California, in the late 1940s. The Radar Navigator Bomb School at Mather AFB near Sacramento used the World War II–era B-25J bombers to train new bomber crews. Training sites such as the Beale Bomb and Gunnery Range helped build the foundations of USAF's new bomber forces.

US Army engineer officers assigned to SCARWAF socialize with local Marysville businessmen. Warren N. Shingles (in white), president of the Marysville Chamber of Commerce, was the man most responsible for establishing Camp Beale, which later became Beale AFB. Fourteenth Street on base was renamed in his honor. W.L. Sears, manager of the Gibson Bus Depot, stands at the far right.

The Headquarters, 1905th Engineer Aviation Battalion (1905 EAB), 136 EAB, Beale Bomb and Gunnery Range is seen as it looked in 1951. The first engineer aviation battalions of the 136 EAB had to set up tent cities until they could build new dormitories.

The USAF was a desegregated service by the 1950s. The men in this image, which shows outdoor wash facilities in the 1905 EAB tent city area in 1951, would not have been allowed to share the same facilities six years prior under the Army Air Forces. The desegregation of the US armed forces removed a major obstacle to building the teamwork needed to face the challenges of the Cold War.

Company B, 832nd Engineer Aviation Battalion (832 EAB), was assigned Test Project 301-55-T to test the performance of the Mississippi Road Service (MRS) 150 tractor for possible fielding to all engineer aviation organizations. This MRS 150 tractor is leveling ground to set up the 50-ton rock crusher unit behind it.

Here, an engineer shaves under field conditions, using a steel helmet and a crate as a washbasin. Conducting field training at Beale AFB allowed the engineers to experience hot, dry, dusty weather most of the year and heavy rains and mud in the winter. Rattlesnakes, ticks, black widow spiders, skunks, coyotes, and mountain lions added to the fun.

The 832 EAB was assigned to Project 305-55-C, construction of airfield phase one, between October 11 and 28, 1954. This project required the construction of a 12,000-foot heavy bomber runway parallel to Best Slough Creek. The Lofton Cemetery, which this image looks towards, is several hundred yards to the south.

A water distributor gives the fill a shot of water during the airfield construction. More than 40,000 square feet of soil had been leveled before this project was abandoned. The main runway of Beale AFB would have been at this location had the project been completed. This would have made the layout of the base completely different from what it is today.

The 832 EAB was assigned Project 301-53-D, rehabilitation of roads and bridges, between October 18, 1954, and April 1, 1955. The view in this image, looking south, shows a Caterpillar D-8 bulldozer pulling a scraper while building the J Street extension from Fourteenth Street (present-day Warren Shingles Street) to the Marysville Road (present-day Doolittle Drive). This extension connected the West Cantonment to the North Cantonment.

Engineers install two 24-inch concrete culverts along a spot where the J Street extension will cross before connecting to the Marysville Road. This scene is near present-day Gate 8, which accesses the flight line. The buildings in the center are the remains of the Camp Beale Station Hospital, built in 1942, which had comprised the North Cantonment. The two-story white building on the right was the hospital steam plant.

The Lake Beale Bridge was built over Dry Creek on the Spenceville-Wheatland Road (present-day Camp Beale Highway) near the former Camp Beale Swimming Pool renamed Lake Beale. This image shows the south abutment nearing completion, with the form for the concrete footer being built at its foundation. The original Spenceville-Wheatland Road in the background was a typical dirt-and-gravel road found throughout Beale AFB at this time.

Company B, 832 EAB, was assigned Project 344-54-L, mess hall paving and drainage in the East Cantonment (present-day Main Base). The earthwork was accomplished on December 17, 1954. This image shows a grader in the foreground working to level out the area to provide a paved road and servicing area. The day after this photograph was taken, heavy rains put a stop to this project.

The motor pool areas in the East Cantonment located between A and B Streets required their earthwork to be stabilized after a decade of abandonment. A scraper levels the final layers of fill on Motor Pool No. 7 before paving. Note the markings "CONAC AEF 832EAB B 49" above the front wheel. This stands for Continental Air Command, Aviation Engineer Force, 832nd Engineer Aviation Battalion, Company B, Vehicle 49.

This image shows the site of a completed motor pool in 1954. Today, this site is used by the current transportation unit as part of its motor pool facility. The building in the foreground has been renovated over the years but is still in use. The buildings in the background are on the site of the present-day 9th Civil Engineering Squadron area.

The remains of M38A1 practice bombs collected from Target No. 1 and Night Target No. 1 of the Beale Bomb and Gunnery Range are designated Stack No. 1 by the explosive ordnance disposal (EOD) teams tasked to clean up the ranges.

An EOD team clears M38A1 practice bomb debris from a target area.

Chow time! The EOD men take a break to have a lunch of Van Camp's chili con carne, Campbell's bean soup with bacon strips, and a can of Spam. They have made a stove by digging a fire pit and are using a commercial outdoor camping grill.

Stack No. 5 consisted of T-63 practice bombs collected by EOD teams clearing the area around Navy Target T-63.

Two

BUILDING THE FLIGHT LINE

On April 13, 1957, the ground-breaking ceremony for the 12,000-foot runway at Beale AFB was conducted by Air Force and local Californian officials. The runway would be located parallel to the site of the former Camp Beale North Cantonment. Flight line facilities would be located about a mile north. The runway and taxi ramp would effectively cut the old Marysville Road between its intersection with J Street and the Camp Beale Highway (present-day North Beale Road). The Main Gate, or Gate No. 1, was relocated west to the intersection with the Camp Beale Highway. The Camp Beale Highway was extended to Erle Road (present-day Gavin Mandery Drive) to allow traffic access on and off the base via the south end of the runway.

The flight line facilities would be designed to support B-52 bombers and KC-135 tankers. Four massive nose dock hangars were built to perform indoor maintenance and an alert facility to house aircrews on alert status. Other facilities supported the Air-to-Ground Missile 28 (AGM-28) Hound Dog nuclear cruise missile carried under the inner-wing pylons of the B-52s.

The nerve center of the flight line operations would be the consolidate building containing the wing headquarters, the command post, the flight line fire department, the chow hall, and field and avionic maintenance shops.

The flight line was completed after 16 months of construction and opened on August 27, 1958. Brig. Gen. Charles M. Eisenhart, commander, 14th Air Division, landed the first aircraft on the runway, a C-47 transport, followed by Maj. Gen. Archie Old Jr., commander, 15th Air Force, landing a VC-97 transport.

The 4126th Strategic Wing (4126 SW) was activated on February 8, 1959, at Beale AFB with Lt. Col. Floyd R. Creasman as the acting wing commander until Col. Paul K. Carlton assumed command on May 15 of that year. The first KC-135 (KC-135A S/N: 58-0071) arrived on July 7, 1959, and was christened the *Spirit of Sacramento Valley* on July 10. The 4126 SW became combat ready on November 1, 1959, with eight KC-135As assigned to the 903rd Air Refueling Squadron (903 ARS).

The two images here show the construction of the 12,000-foot runway at Beale AFB on June 12, 1957. This part of Beale AFB had the most level land and contributed to its site selection. However, several hills still had to be removed or excavated to complete the project.

Rails are laid and heavy machinery is brought in to pour the concrete slabs for the 12,000-foot runway. The machines to the left and middle pour the concrete into the forms. The machine on the right levels the concrete.

Shown here is a close-up of the machines used to pour the concrete.

The two images here show the air traffic control tower under construction.

The buildings on the flight line are starting to take shape in this photograph. In the foreground is the air traffic control tower; the base operations building is directly behind it. The steel frames for the nose dock hangars have been built. The red-and-white-checkered water tower stands in the background. Today, all these structures remain except for the control tower, which was demolished and replaced by the present-day tower.

Shown here are the air traffic control tower and base operations as they looked upon completion.

The site of the new consolidated building near the flight line has been leveled and the ground excavated for the command post. The building will contain the wing headquarters, command post, maintenance facilities, a chow hall, fire department, life support shop, and test and evaluation shop when completed.

This photograph shows the new Runway 33 and flight line of Beale AFB as seen before it became operational in August 27, 1958. This view is looking north. Runway 33 becomes Runway 15 when viewed from the north looking south.

This view shows the completed nose dock hangars. To the left is the consolidated building, complete with its parachute-rigging tower for the life support unit.

The flight line facilities in September 1962 are seen from the north end. The structures shown are, from front to back, the AGM-28 engine maintenance test area, the three-building AGM-28 maintenance facilities, the field maintenance squadron, the operational maintenance squadron headquarters, the consolidated building, the four nose dock hangars, and the air traffic control tower and operations building. On the flight line are B-52E bombers.

The original Main Gate, or Gate No. 1 (Building T-2153), was built in 1943 and was based on the main gate at Camp Hann, California. The *T* in the building number indicates it was a temporary structure. The gate was located on the Marysville Road (present-day Doolittle Drive) connecting Marysville with Spenceville prior to Camp Beale being built. This view is looking west from the outbound lane in December 1952.

The Main Gate had to be relocated due to the construction of the runway. The Camp Beale Highway (present-day North Beale Road) was extended to Erle Road (present-day Gavin Mandery Drive), enabling traffic to round the south end of the runway. The site of the new main gate was placed where the Marysville Road had once intersected with the Camp Beale Highway.

The first Beale Air Force Base Main Gate is seen here upon completion. The sign above the gate reads, "Beale Air Force Base, Home of the 14th Strategic Aerospace Division." The aircraft silhouettes show a KC-135 tanker flying above a B-52. The 14th Strategic Aerospace Division patch is in the upper left corner.

This sign was located in front of the headquarters of the 14th Air Division. The 14th Strategic Aerospace Division was re-designated the 14th Air Division on March 31, 1972.

KC-135A S/N: 58-0071 was the first KC-135 assigned to the 903 ARS, 4126 SW, at Beale AFB. It was christened the *Spirit of Sacramento Valley* and flew a 600-mile round-trip mission to refuel B-52 bombers on July 10, 1959. From left to right are Col. Paul K. Carlton, commander, 4126 SW, and that day's mission commander; Capt. James L. Sharpley, aircraft commander; Maj. Walter B. Remington, instructor pilot; 1st Lt. P.K. Foley, copilot; Maj. John J. Brinkley, navigator; MSgt. Carl Lewis Jr., boom operator; and TSgt. Newman J. Dixon, crew chief. Colonel Carlton later presented Major Remington with a pin acknowledging that he was the first aircrew member in SAC to have completed 2,000 flying hours in a KC-135 aircraft.

Three

TITAN I MISSILE SITES

The HGM-25A Titan I nuclear missile was the first multistage intercontinental ballistic missile (ICBM) the United States built. The first successful launch was conducted on February 5, 1959. The Titan I would be the first strategic missile deployed in what would become the nuclear defense triad, which utilized bombers, missiles, and submarines. It carried a 3.75-megaton W38 thermonuclear warhead.

SAC deployed the missile across six missile squadrons in five states. Each squadron would have three missile sites under its command with three missile silos at each site. The 4126 SW at Beale AFB would receive one of these missile squadrons. The three sites would be located near Lincoln (Complex 4-A), Sutter Buttes (Complex 4-B), and Chico (Complex 4-C). Construction began in January 1960. Over 600,000 cubic yards of earth had to be excavated and backfilled at each site. The facilities consisted of three silos, a control center, a powerhouse, and two antenna silos. Aboveground, two Quonset huts and prefab buildings were built for maintenance and contractor support.

The 851st Strategic Missile Squadron (851 SMS) was activated on February 1, 1961, under the command of Col. William L. Reynolds. The first Titan I missile arrived at Beale AFB on January 12, 1962, and was installed at the Complex 4-A on February 28. The last missile was installed on April 20 at Complex 4-C. A massive explosion on May 24, destroyed Missile Silo No. 1 at Complex 4-C and delayed the site from becoming fully operational until March 9, 1963. The 851 SMS was placed on alert status in September 1962.

The Titan I was not an ideal weapon system. The missiles had to be raised out of their silos and fueled aboveground before being launched. This made them vulnerable to a nuclear attack. The secretary of defense ordered the deactivation of the Titan I program on May 16, 1964. The first missile at Beale AFB was taken off alert status on January 4, 1965, and the last missile was removed and shipped to depot by February 10. The 851 SMS was deactivated on March 25, 1965.

The Titan I Missile Facility T-5, Complex 4-C, is being constructed near Chico, California, in this image. All three missile sites were identically constructed, with over 600,000 cubic yards of earth excavated and backfilled at each location. Complex 4-A, near Lincoln, California, was physically the closest to a populated area and Complex 4-B, near Sutter Buttes, California, was the most isolated. The site names used here come from official documents from both 4126th Strategic Wing and 456th Strategic Aerospace Wing that identified the sites.

This image shows the powerhouse of Complex 4-B in the foreground, the control center in the middle, and the equipment terminal to the far left as it is under construction. Shockproof tunnels will connect all the site facilities. All these structures will be buried out of sight once completed.

The antenna silos are under construction at Complex 4-B. The antenna silo guided the initial trajectory of the Titan I missile when launched. One of the serious flaws with the Titan I sites was that only one missile could be guided to target at a time by the antenna silo. This left the other two missiles awaiting launch vulnerable to an attack.

This image, taken on March 22, 1961, shows the powerhouse of the Complex 4-C as it nears completion. The dome shape of the structure will allow it to withstand the blast effects of a nuclear attack.

The interior door of Blast Lock No. 2 at Complex 4-C is shown with one of the shockproof connecting tunnels. The ribbed walls allow the tunnel to move with a shock wave and minimize any damage.

One of the interior facilities at Complex 4-A, seen in this image, has been completed and is awaiting furnishings.

A Titan I missile is transported from Beale AFB to Complex 4-A under a white tarp on April 13, 1962.

The first stage of Titan I S/N: 60-3688 is raised from its transport by electrical crane to be lowered into its silo at Complex 4-A. Electrical cranes where not commonplace at this time in history. The raising and lowering of the missiles were practiced in the parking lot of the Base Theater at Beale AFB using telephone poles. The telephone poles were slowly lowered onto a paper cup until the crews could do it without crushing the cup.

Shown here is another image of the first stage of Titan I S/N: 60-3688 being lowered into its silo at Complex 4-A. The use of an electrical crane allowed for a very smooth, steady, and precise movement of the missile.

The second stage of Titan I S/N: 60-3688 is about to be lowered into its silo at Complex 4-A in this photograph.

Titan I S/N: 60-3688 is fully assembled and shown aboveground in launch position at Complex 4-A. The Titan I missile had to be raised by elevators aboveground before it could be fueled. This practice wasted valuable time and made the missile highly vulnerable to a nuclear attack.

A B-52 bomber from the 31st Bombardment Squadron, 4126 SW, makes passes over Complex 4-C while a Titan I is raised at the launch position.

This image was taken from the same B-52 bomber shown on the previous page as it flew over Complex 4-C.

Three Titan I missiles are shown aboveground in launch positions at Complex 4-C.

A prelaunch test on May 24, 1962, went wrong at Complex 4-C, Missile Silo No. 1. A small explosion occurred, followed by a massive explosion that destroyed the silo, the missile, and all support equipment. The damage was over $8.6 million. This aerial image was taken on the afternoon of the event.

Blockages of the liquid oxygen (LOX) fill blast valve and ventilation systems allowed gaseous oxygen (GOX) to build up. A small explosion occurred and the entire complex was evacuated at 0645 hours. This was followed by a massive explosion that ripped through the silo and showered debris across the complex. A tank of unknown liquefied gas was ruptured by the explosion and the trailer it was on damaged.

Shown here is debris left on top of Missile Silo No. 1 from the explosion. Note the thickness of the concrete. The North Gate guard nearly missed being seriously injured or killed when a 500-pound piece of metal landed near him. The blast reached the surface through one of the exhaust vents and showered the surface compound with debris that damaged several facilities.

This image shows one of two Quonset huts that were severely damaged by the blast.

Col. Bernard Garfinkel, deputy commander of the 851 SMS, conducts an on-site briefing for the incoming crew in January 1964.

Unidentified 851 SMS missile crewmen pose for a group photograph in January 1964. From left to right, the ranks are sergeant, three staff sergeants, captain, and major. The officers were the ones responsible for the actual launching of the missiles, should the order come down from the president.

The missile sites of the 851 SMS were ordered to close down in 1965 as the Titan I was replaced by the Titan II. This image was taken on February 23, 1965, and shows the second stage of a Titan I missile at Complex 4-A being lowered onto an A-frame prior to shipment to a depot.

In this photograph, the final adjustments are made on a Titan I during the pre-shipment inspection.

Four

KC-135 STRATOTANKER

The 903rd Air Refueling Squadron (903 ARS) was the first KC-135 unit assigned to Beale AFB. Its first aircraft, KC-135A S/N: 58-0071, arrived on July 7, 1959. The unit started with KC-135As and transitioned to the KC-135Qs with the arrival of the SR-71 units at Beale AFB in 1965. The primary mission of the 903 ARS was to provide aerial refueling for the wing's B-52 bombers. Two KC-135s were always on alert status. The 903 ARS carried out this mission for 17 years with three different bomb squadrons under four different wings until June 30, 1976, when the bomber mission at Beale AFB came to an end.

The 9th Air Refueling Squadron (9 ARS) was activated at Beale AFB on January 1, 1970, as part of the 456th Strategic Aerospace Wing (456 SAW). The unit was equipped with KC-135Qs and supported both the B-52s and SR-71s at the base. The 9 ARS was deactivated June 30, 1976, along with the bomb wing and was re-designated the 349th Air Refueling Squadron (349 ARS) under the 100th Air Refueling Wing (100 ARW), which took over as the host wing at Beale AFB. The 349 ARS was joined by the 350th Air Refueling Squadron (350 ARS) on January 28, 1982, and both squadrons became known as the "Beale Bandits." The 100 ARW was deactivated on March 15, 1983, and the 9th Strategic Reconnaissance Wing became the host wing at Beale AFB, incorporating both the 349 ARS and 350 ARS. The Beale Bandits supplemented Military Airlift Command's (MAC) airlift fleet during Operation Desert Shield/Desert Storm.

The 349 ARS was deactivated on June 5, 1992. This left the 350 ARS as the last SAC air refueling squadron at Beale AFB until July 1, 1994, when it transferred to McConnell AFB, Kansas, under the new Air Mobility Command (AMC). The KC-135 was the first SAC aircraft to arrive at Beale AFB and it was the last SAC aircraft to leave. Its mission at Beale AFB lasted 35 years and 6 days; it outlasted all other SAC aircraft missions at the base.

Shown here is the KC-135 parking ramp area at Beale AFB. A B-52G is taking off in the background.

A KC-135A of the 903 ARS, 456 SAW, is being washed by administrative personnel during a Mission Standardization Evaluation and Training (MSET) inspection sometime between January and March 1967.

KC-135Q S/N: 58-0112 is parked near the entrance of the parking ramp at Beale AFB as an intruder breaches the security perimeter.

Security Forces quickly apprehended any unauthorized personnel entering restricted areas around the aircraft. This is a publicity photograph. The reality would have the individual face down on the ground, spread-eagled, with the barrel of an M-16 aimed at the back of his head while being handcuffed. The use of deadly force was authorized to protect all aircraft.

KC-135Q S/N: 58-0120 is seen on the ramp at Beale AFB following a heavy rainstorm. The KC-135Q models were converted KC-135A models with dual valves installed in them to allow the forward and aft fuel tanks to be separated from the remaining fuel tanks. This enabled the tankers to carry JP-7 fuel used by the SR-71 while separating the JP-4 fuel used by the KC-135.

This photograph shows KC-135Q S/N: 59-1520 on the parking ramp; the consolidated building is in the background.

KC-135Q S/N: 60-0339 is shown here in the parking area. The nose art depicts the Warner Bros. cartoon character Yosemite Sam inside a large white letter Q. Yosemite Sam represented the Beale Bandits nickname used by both the 349 ARS and 350 ARS. Crew patches and aircraft nose art for both units regularly displayed his image.

KC-135Q S/N: 60-0339 is seen landing on the south end of the Runway 33.

KC-135Q S/N: 59-1513 is taking off near the south end of the Runway 15 in this photograph.

In this image, KC-135Q S/N: 58-0143 is landing on the north end of Runway 15.

KC-135Q S/N: 59-1471, 9 SRW, is shown here, displaying the Sutter Buttes overlooking the Yuba River, with the steamboat *Linda* sailing upstream.

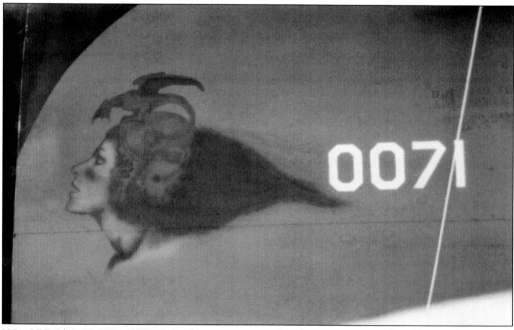

KC-135Q S/N: 58-0071, 9 SRW, displays a woman with a dragon ornament headdress. This aircraft was originally KC-135A, *Spirit of Sacramento Valley*, which is shown on page 28. It was converted to a Q model sometime after the SR-71 program arrived at Beale AFB in 1965.

Jezebel, KC-135Q S/N: 58-0074, 9 SRW, is shown here, displaying Jessica Rabbit from the movie *Who Framed Roger Rabbit*.

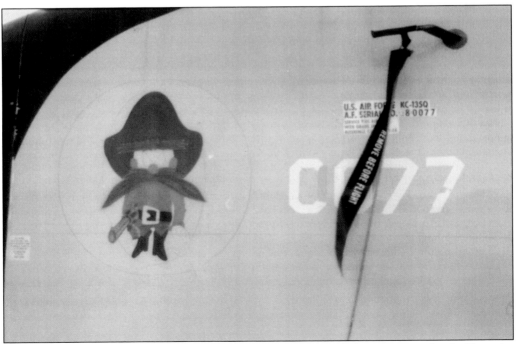

KC-135Q S/N: 58-0077, 9 SRW, is displaying a work in progress of what appears to be the Yosemite Sam character standing inside the letter Q.

An Old West scene of a Native American on horse back watching the sunset is seen on KC-135Q
S/N: 60-342, 9 SRW.

KC-135Q S/N: 59-1460, 9 SRW displays an American bald eagle soaring through the sky.

KC-135Q S/N: 58-0103, 9 SRW, is seen flying over the Sacramento Valley.

This photograph shows KC-135Q S/N: 58-074, 9 SRW, flying over Lake Tahoe. This is the same aircraft, *Jezebel*, shown at the top of page 50 after receiving a new olive drab paint scheme, replacing the grey two-tone paint scheme.

Five

B-52 Stratofortress

The 31st Bombardment Squadron (31 BS) transferred from Travis AFB, California, to Beale AFB on January 18, 1960, with its 12 B-52E bombers. This was part of SAC's plan to disperse its strategic nuclear strike capabilities in the event of a sudden attack by the Soviet Union. The 14th Air Division also transferred from Travis AFB to Beale AFB on January 25, 1960. The B-52Es operated up through 1962 at Beale AFB before they were replaced by B-52Gs.

Universal Pictures received the full support of the United States Air Force in making a film about SAC. Studio representatives and Beale AFB officials met in April 1962 to plan out the filming schedule under the code name Operation Birdleg. The movie *A Gathering of Eagles* was filmed primarily at Beale AFB and stars Rock Hudson, Rod Taylor, and Mary Peach. Filming began on the aerial sequences on June 25, 1962. The stars arrived at Beale AFB on July 16 and filmed for six weeks. The most dramatic scene in the movie is the Minimal Interval Takeoff (MITO), in which Rock Hudson and Rod Taylor stand by Runway 15 and time the launch of B-52 bombers scrambling. The film crew was so grateful for the support it received that Universal Pictures donated a swimming pool to the alert facility and a roller-skating rink to the main base.

The 4126 SW was re-designated the 456th Strategic Aerospace Wing (456 SAW) and the 31 BS was re-designated the 744th Bombardment Squadron (744 BS) on February 1, 1963. Some B-52Ds were incorporated into the wing sometime in the late 1960s. The designation of the wing would again change on July 1, 1972, when the 456 SAW was re-designated the 456th Bombardment Wing, Heavy [456 BW(H)]. The strategic nuclear bombing mission at Beale AFB ended when both the 456 BW(H) and the 744 BS were deactivated and replaced by the 17th Bombardment Wing (17 BW) and the 34th Bombardment Squadron (34 BS) on September 30, 1975. The B-52Gs flew training missions until the 17 BW and 34 BS were deactivated on June 30, 1976.

A B-52E bomber, 31 BS, 4126 SW, does a flyby over the south end of the runway in front of a crowd of Boy Scouts, civilians, and military personnel. The first four B-52E bombers of the 31 BS arrived from Travis AFB on January 18, 1960. The 14th Air Division followed on January 25, 1960.

The first AGM-28 Hound Dog nuclear cruise missile arrived at Beale AFB on August 25, 1961, and was assigned to the 31 BS, 4126 SW. This close-up image of two missiles of the 744 BS, 456 SAW, was taken in 1969. Note the SAC emblem and the Milky Way banner near the warhead.

These are two photographs showing six AGM-28 nuclear cruise missiles sitting in front of the AGM-28 engine maintenance facility in 1969. The missiles were painted depending on the paint scheme of the aircraft they were assigned to.

B-52G S/N: 57-6491, 744 BS, 456 SAW, is sitting alert in 1969 in the parking ramp area of the Beale AFB flight line. It is armed with two AGM-28 nuclear cruise missiles attached to the inner wing pylons. In the background to the left are the AGM-28 maintenance facilities.

B-52G S/N: 57-6480 is shown here on the flight line of Beale AFB. This photograph clearly shows the high gloss, anti-flash white underside paint scheme that was adopted by the SAC's bomber fleet to reflect a nuclear flash and heat away from the bomber. This bomber ended up at Aerospace Maintenance and Regeneration Center (AMARC), row 29, on August 5, 1992, to be scrapped.

Five B-52G bombers line the Beale AFB flight line at night in 1969. The aircraft in the foreground is B-52G S/N: 59-2597, 744 BS, 456 SAW.

The tail sections of four B-52G bombers of the 744 BS are clearly seen displaying the Avco-Crosley AN/ASG-15 defensive fire control system mounting four .50 caliber machine guns. The gunner sat with the electronic warfare officer (EWO) and monitored threats via radar and a television monitor. The first three aircraft are, from front to back, B-52G S/N: 57-6515, B-52G S/N: 57-8477, and B-52G S/N: 58-0184.

The camera crew from Universal Pictures takes a break while waiting to film a scene at Beale AFB in July 1962 for the movie *A Gathering of Eagles*. The film stars Rock Hudson and Rod Taylor as two officers of the Strategic Air Command preparing a bomb wing to pass an Operational Readiness Inspection (ORI).

The officers' wives orientation scene from *A Gathering of Eagles* was filmed in the auditorium of the recreation center. Today, this facility is known as the Community Activity Center (CAC). The auditorium has changed little from its July 1962 appearance in the film. All the extras in the scene are actual Beale AFB officers' wives at the time.

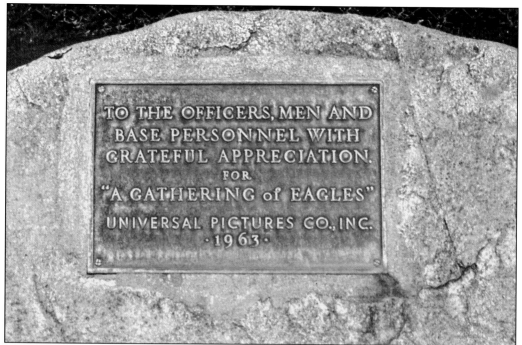

Universal Pictures was so grateful for the support it received in making A *Gathering of Eagles* that it had a swimming pool built in the alert facility area for the airmen. The dedication plaque near the entrance to the pool had the following inscription: "To the officers, men, and base personnel with grateful appreciation. For 'A Gathering of Eagles' Universal Pictures Co. Inc. 1963." The swimming pool was closed and filled in when the alert facility was no longer required at Beale AFB.

Maintenance personnel are preparing B-52G S/N: 59-2596, 744 BS, 456 SAW, for a mission while her crew members wait in the bomber's shade prior to boarding.

A B-52G of the 744 BS, 456 SAW, flies by the ground-controlled approach unit of the Air Force Communication Service (AFCS) facility at Beale AFB on March 13, 1970.

Six

SCRAMBLE!

The alert facility was located on the north end of the flight line next to the "Christmas Tree," where the alert aircraft were parked and ready to scramble. The alert facility consisted of offices, a dining room with kitchen, a theater/briefing room, a library, and a recreation room on the first level. The lower levels contained the single or double-occupancy dorm rooms based on rank and title. The center hallways contained the common latrines with showers. There was a combination basketball/volleyball court outdoors on the flight line side of the building.

Klaxons were installed throughout Beale AFB. The aircrews in the alert facility physically ran to their aircraft parked nearby when the Klaxons sounded. Those aircrew members away from the facility responded in alert vehicles and parked them on the basketball/volleyball court. The B-52 electronic warfare officers (EWO) and gunners had the responsibility of removing the engine covers and wheel chalks while the rest of the crew started up the aircraft. The KC-135s were the quickest to start up and usually the first to roll out. The Christmas Tree opened directly onto the north end of Runway 15.

The goal was to have all alert aircraft airborne within 15 minutes. The MITO created a dangerous situation for aircraft heavily loaded with fuel and bombs. They would have to take off into the jet wash of the aircraft in front of them. The aircraft fanned out as they climbed to help minimize the amount of turbulence the follow-on aircraft had to fly through. One Mather AFB aircraft and crew was lost during the Cold War performing a MITO scramble. B-52s carrying the AGM-28s could use the missile engines to provide additional thrust to get airborne. B-52s that used the AGM-28s for assistance refueled the missiles at cruise altitude from their internal fuel tanks. The B-52s then rendezvoused with the KC-135s and refueled before heading to their targets.

Today, the alert facility and Christmas Tree still remain. The alert facility has undergone significant renovations and no longer resembles its Cold War layout.

The front of the alert facility at the north end of the flight line was where aircrews on alert status lived. This facility provided living quarters, a dining room and kitchen, a recreation room, a library, a theater/briefing room, and a combination basketball/volleyball court. The alert facilities were standardized structures found throughout SAC at all Air Force bases supporting America's nuclear bomber forces during the Cold War.

The flight line side of the alert facility with the combination basketball/volleyball court is shown in the foreground. The first floor contained the offices and common facilities and the lower levels held the living quarters.

The alert facility had its own dining room and kitchen. The post–Cold War use of the building did not require these facilities, causing them to be removed.

Aircrew members are relaxing in the alert facility's library at Beale AFB. This library no longer exists.

The dorm rooms were located in the lower levels of the alert facility and housed either single occupancy or double occupancy depending on rank and duty titles. Officers and enlisted men were separated. Common latrines and showers were in the central hallways.

Klaxon! A captain scrambles from his alert vehicle he has just parked on the basketball/volleyball court of the alert facility at Beale AFB. Aircrews on alert status had alert vehicles assigned to them to quickly respond in the event their duties took them away from the alert facility. The badge on the left breast pocket of the onlooker with headphones identifies him as a member of the Security Forces.

KC-135A aircrew members of the 4126th Strategic Wing at Beale AFB scramble to their aircraft. The KC-135 tankers were the quickest to start up and get airborne and were usually parked the closest to the alert facility, shown in the background.

The front landing gear is starting to lift off the runway on this KC-135 from the 903 ARS as the tanker races down Runway 15 on Beale AFB.

The collage here shows a KC-135 racing down Runway 15 from the north and then taking off to the south.

Two KC-135s from the 903 ARS get airborne near the south end of Runway 15 at Beale AFB during a scramble.

Two KC-135s from the 903 ARS fan out as they climb into the skies of Northern California during a scramble from Beale AFB. Fanning out was an important maneuver to lessen the amount of turbulence from the aircraft in front that the following aircraft had to fly through.

Through rain or shine, the strategic bomber crews of the 31 BS and 744 BS were ready to scramble. The EWO and the tail gunner had the duties of removing covers from engines and the chalks from the wheels while the rest of the crew was going through the start-up procedures to get their bomber moving.

B-52G S/N: 57-6486, 744 BS, 456 SAW, scrambles down Runway 33 during an Exercise Bar None around 1964, carrying two AGM-28 cruise missiles. The jet engines on the AGM-28s could be activated to assist the bomber on takeoff. The bombers would refill the fuel tanks of the missiles once airborne and at altitude. They would then rendezvous with the KC-135s to have their own fuel tanks filled up.

Reminiscent of a scene from the movie A *Gathering of Eagles*, the wing commander and his staff look on as B-52G S/N: 59-2567, 744 BS, 456 SAW, roars past them down Runway 15 during an Exercise Bar None scramble around 1964. The aircraft is carrying two AGM-28 cruise missiles.

B-52G S/N: 58-2586, 744 BS, 456 SAW, is scrambling down Runway 15 during an Operational Readiness Inspection (ORI) sometime between January and March 1967.

A K-9 patrol provides flight line security as a B-52G scrambles into the sky at sunset.

Shown here is a B-52G rendezvous with a KC-135 along the coast of Northern California. A scramble used up a lot of fuel to get the bomb-laden B-52s airborne. Aerial refueling was critical to ensure the bombers could reach their targets.

The B-52G closes the distance to the K-135 in this photograph.

This is the view the boom operator has of the approaching B-52G, including a spectacular scene of the coast of Northern California below.

This is the view the pilot has while approaching the boom of a KC-135 to refuel.

The fuel receptacle can clearly be seen on the roof behind the cockpit of the B-52G as it closes the distance to the boom.

A KC-135 tanker from the 903 ARS refuels a B-52G of the 744 BS in skies above Northern California.

Seven

VIETNAM WAR

The 456 SAW started deploying aircrews in 1968 to support the KC-135 "Young Tiger" missions and the B-52 "Arc Light II" missions over Southeast Asia. The 456 SAW fully deployed in 1972. Midway through this deployment, the 456 SAW was re-designated the 456 BW. The Beale B-52 aircrews and maintenance personnel were deployed to the 307th Strategic Wing (307 SW), 3rd Air Division, in support of combat operations over Southeast Asia in early 1972. The wing's B-52Ds were stationed at U-Tapao Royal Thai Air Base (RTAB), Thailand, and its B-52Gs at Anderson Air Base, Guam, with the 307 SW Provisional (307 SW(P)). The Beale aircrews saw their first combat missions as part of Operation Bullet Shot during the Arc Light II bombing campaign. The bombing missions over Vietnam, Laos, and Cambodia had the aircrews flying in a V formations that was comprised of three aircraft called "Cells" and dropping sticks of 1,000-pound and 750-pound bombs against low-value targets. This was a departure from an alert mission of one aircraft striking high value targets with nuclear weapons.

The air war over Vietnam finally went strategic from December 18 to 29, 1972, when Pres. Richard M. Nixon ordered the heavy bombing of strategic targets in North Vietnam. The official designation of this campaign was Linebacker II, but it became known as the "Christmas Bombings." For the first time in the war, B-52 crews flew into the heart of North Vietnamese air defenses and faced a barrage of Soviet-built Type II surface-to-air missiles (SAM II). The B-52 bombers partaking in Linebacker II would play a powerful role in bringing an end to American involvement in the Vietnam War.

The 456 BW had been successful in carrying out its missions over Southeast Asia. However, those successes were not without loss as two of its B-52 aircrews from the 744 BS made the ultimate sacrifices in the performance of their duties.

CREW R-18

Captain Thomas W. Reasor
KIA July 30, 1972

Captain Ronald A. Ashe
KIA July 30, 1972

Captain David J. Price
KIA July 30, 1972

Captain Joseph L. Ruzicka, Jr.
KIA July 30, 1972

Major James E. Hudelson
KIA July 30, 1972

> **Master Sergeant Eugene C. Gries**
> **RESCUED July 20, 1972**
> **Since retired—no photo available**

B-52D S/N: 56-0677, 744 BS, 456 BW, was deployed to the 307 SW at U-Tapao RTAB, Thailand. On July 30, 1972, this aircraft was assigned to Mission R-18 and was crewed by Capt. Thomas W. Reasor, aircraft commander; Capt. Ronald A. Ashe, copilot; Capt. David J. Price, radar navigator; Capt. Joseph L. Ruzicka Jr., navigator; Maj. James E. Hudelson, EWO; and MSgt. Eugene C. Gries, tail gunner. B-52D S/N: 56-0677 was hit by lightning while en route to its target. The strike knocked out all instrumentation and sent the aircraft plummeting from the sky near At Samat in the Roi Et Province of Thailand. Captain Ruzicka and Master Sergeant Gries ejected before the bomber crashed. Captain Ruzicka was fatally injured. Master Sergeant Gries survived. A memorial service was held in Chapel Two at Beale AFB on August 4, 1972, to honor the R-18 crewmen killed in action. Chaplain (Lt. Col.) Beverly J. Barnett gave the eulogy in front of 500 attendees. After the eulogy, a B-52 did a low-level flyover of the chapel. (Photograph by the *Space Sentinel*, Friday, November 23, 1973.)

CREW E-13

Captain Warren R. Spencer

MIA Dec. 20, 1972

Lieutenant Craig A. Paul

MIA Dec. 20, 1972

Captain Terry M. Geloneck

REPATRIATED Feb. 11, 1973

Lieutenant Michael R. Martini

REPATRIATED March 29, 1973

Technical Sergeant Roy Madden, Jr.

REPATRIATED FEB. 11, 1973

Lieutenant William L. Arcuri

REPATRIATED Feb. 11, 1973

B-52G S/N: 57-6492, 744 BS, 456 BW, was deployed to the 307 SW(P), Anderson AB, Guam. On night three of the Linebacker II bombings, December 20, 1972, this aircraft was assigned Mission E-13 and was crewed by Capt. Terry M. Geloneck, aircraft commander; 1st Lt. William Y. Arcuri, copilot; Capt. Warren R. Spencer, radar navigator; 1st Lt. Michael R. Martini, navigator; 1st Lt. Craig A. Paul, EWO; and SSgt. Roy Madden, tail gunner. They flew in the No. 3 position of a three-bomber strike cell, called Quilt Cell, with the call sign Quilt 3. The target was the Yen Ven Rail Yards near Hanoi. Time on target was 2209 hours local when "Bombs Away!" was ordered. Quilt 3 made a 60-degree Post Target Turn (PTT) and was immediately hit by a SAM II. Capt. Geloneck was unable to maintain flight control and ordered the crew to "Bail Out!" Four crewmen ejected with serious injuries and were captured. Captain Spencer and First Lieutenant Paul went down with the bomber. (Photograph by the *Space Sentinel*, Friday, November 23, 1973.)

Operation Homecoming began on February 12, 1973, as the first USAF C-5 cargo plane landed at Hanoi to bring American prisoners of war home. When the C-5 cleared Vietnamese airspace, a thunderous cheer erupted throughout the aircraft in a scene like the one shown here. Captain Geloneck, First Lieutenant Arcuri, and Staff Sergeant Madden from 744 BS, 456 BW, Beale AFB, were on that first flight due to their injuries. Next stop was Clark AB, Philippines, for medical evaluations and debriefings. Staff Sergeant Madden's leg had to be amputated upon reaching US medical facilities at Clark AB. For the crew of E-13, the final trip would be made via a C-141 that landed at Travis AFB, California. First Lieutenant Martini was repatriated on March 29, 1973. Captain Spencer's and First Lieutenant Paul's remains were returned on September 30, 1977. Brig. Gen. John P. Flynn, former POW, is quoted in the Friday, November 23, 1973, *Space Sentinel*: "When SAC B-52s started coming over in the December raids, hardened Navy carrier fighter pilots came up to me and said that for the first time they understood why we have a Strategic Air Command. This was the supreme accolade."

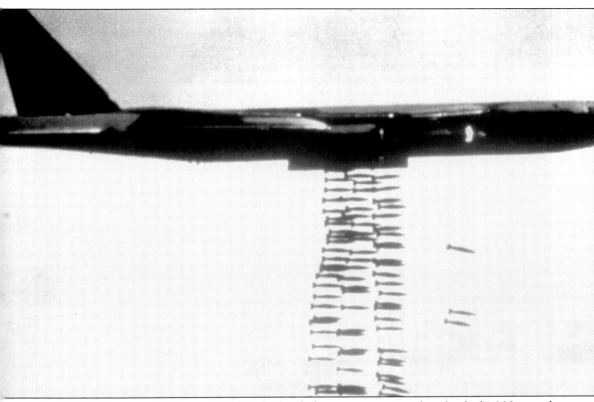

A B-52D flying out of U-Tapao RTAB, Thailand, drops a conventional payload of 1,000-pound and 750-pound bombs somewhere over Vietnam, Laos, or Cambodia. The bombs will wreak havoc across a path two miles long. The underside of the bomber is painted black to protect against detection in searchlights during night operations. The crew of R-18 was flying a similar mission when it was lost on July 30, 1972.

B-52G S/N: 58-0165, 744 BS, 456 BW is seen at Beale AFB. This aircraft was deployed to the 307 SW(P), 3rd Air Division, at Anderson AB, Guam, in 1972 to support combat operations over Southeast Asia. Nineteen years later, it saw combat again, serving with the 801st Bomb Wing Provisional at Moron AB, Spain, during Operation Desert Storm. B-52G S/N: 58-0165 was turned over to the Aerospace Maintenance & Regeneration Center (AMARC) on August 10, 1992.

Families on the home front gather at Travis AFB, California, awaiting the return of their sons, husbands, and fathers during Operation Homecoming.

Eight

SR-71 Blackbird/Habu

The Department of Defense announced the new SR-71 high-altitude reconnaissance aircraft would be stationed at Beale AFB on October 15, 1964. This ushered in a new era of construction at the base as new flight line facilities were built or upgraded. The $8.5 million construction program was given the code name Blue Light Project. A new composite building was constructed on the south side of the nose dock hangars and 12 new hangars were built on the south end of the parking ramp.

The headquarters for SAC issued Special Order G-142 on January 1, 1965, activating the 4200th Strategic Reconnaissance Wing (4200 SRW). The 4200 SRW received its first aircraft, a T-38 companion trainer, on July 8, 1965. The first SR-71 assigned was SR-71B S/N: 61-7957, which arrived at Beale AFB on January 7, 1966. The 4200 SRW was deactivated and replaced by the 9th Strategic Reconnaissance Wing (9 SRW) on June 25, 1966, with the 1st Strategic Reconnaissance Squadron (1 SRS) flying operational missions and the 99th Strategic Reconnaissance Squadron (99 SRW) flying test and training missions. The 99 SRS was deactivated April 1, 1971.

The two forward operating bases for the SR-71 were Operating Location 8 (OL-8), Detachment 1, Kadena Air Base, Okinawa, Japan, and Detachment 4, RAF Mildenhall, United Kingdom. OL-8 received its first SR-71 on March 9, 1968, and was declared operational on March 15. The Okinawans nicknamed the SR-71 the "Habu" after the indigenous pit viper. A white habu was painted on the right side of the aircraft behind the Reconnaissance Systems Operator (RSO) for each mission completed. The SR-71 played a key role in gathering intelligence over Southeast Asia. SR-71 photographs were used to plan the rescue of POWs during the Son Tay prison raid.

The SR-71 established several unbroken world speed records throughout the 1970s and 1980s. The SR-71 fleet was retired after 25 years of flying at Beale AFB on January 26, 1990. Detachment 2, 9 SRW, was activated at Edwards AFB, California, with three SR-71s on April 1, 1995. The SR-71 program came to a final end on March 6, 1998.

SR-71B S/N 61-7956, 1 SRS, 9 SRW, is seen taxiing in front of the SR-71 hangars at Beale AFB.

This SR-71 is taxiing out from Hangar 116 (Building 962) at Beale AFB.

SR-71A S/N: 61-7974, *Ichi-ban*, is seen rotating back to Beale AFB in 1968 after its first tour at OL-8, 9 SRW, Kadena Air Base, Okinawa, Japan. *Ichi-ban* had completed the most missions in the 9 SRW at the time. TSgt. Don Person, crew chief, pointed this out by painting the tail art of a large white habu behind a red *1* and the red words *ichi-ban* ("number one" in Japanese) below.

TSgt. Michael Haggerty of the 1352nd Audio Visual Squadron (1352 AVS) at Norton AFB, California, captured this image of SR-71A, 1 SRS, 9 SRW, Beale AFB, flying over Northern California on June 1, 1988. (Photograph by TSgt. Michael Haggerty, 1352 AVS/DOOJ, Norton AFB, California.)

SR-71A S/N: 61-7962 is seen here as it takes off from Runway 15, heading south on a training mission.

This photograph shows SR-71A S/N: 61-7962 landing on Runway 15; the Sutter Buttes are in the background.

SR-71A S/N: 61-7962 is taxiing down the parking ramp at Beale AFB between KC-135Q tankers and B-52G bombers in this image.

SR-71A S/N: 61-7962 returns to Beale AFB from a flight. The Sutter Buttes can be partially seen to the left in the background, while a KC-135Q comes in for a landing in the upper right. SR-71A S/N: 61-7962 is now on display at the Imperial War Museum at Duxford, England. It is the only SR-71 on display outside the continental United States.

Seen here is a SR-71 parked in its hangar at Beale AFB. Note the blast fence outside the hangar behind the aircraft.

The cowlings on the engine compartment of the SR-71 seen in this image are opened to allow maintainers easier access to the engine.

This is a rare image of maintenance being performed on the SR-71, with the engine spike removed on the right engine. The maintainer is doing a thorough inspection to check for stress, cracks, and to ensure there are no foreign objects that could damage the engine in flight. The SR-71's ability to reach Mach 3.5 meant the engines had to be in pristine condition to avoid a catastrophic failure.

This photograph shows a rear view of the engine compartment with the engine removed. Note the jacks that are in place to prevent the aircraft from tipping over.

A SR-71 streaks into the sky, with the Main Gate in the foreground. The photographer was documenting structures on Beale AFB and photographing the Main Gate when this opportunity presented itself. Note that the sign above the gate now includes an image of a SR-71 along with a KC-135 and B-52, as compared to the sign in the image at the top of page 27.

T-38A S/N: 64-13194 and T-38A S/N: 64-13270 are seen in the T-38 parking area at the north end of the parking ramp. The original T-38As assigned to the 4200 SRW and 9 SRW were painted overall white with a black antiglare strip on the top of the nose. The numbers and lettering were painted in black. The SAC emblem was displayed on the left tail flash only.

This T-38 belonging to the 9 SRW is displaying silhouettes of a U-2 and SR-71 on its speed brakes. Displaying artwork on the T-38 speed brakes was a common practice during this period at Beale AFB.

The D-21 drone was originally designed to be launched from two modified A-12 Blackbirds (S/Ns: 60-6940 and 60-6941), designated M-21s, that carried the drones piggyback. The fourth test launch on June 30, 1966, resulted in the drone colliding with M-21 S/N: 60-6941 and the loss of the aircraft and one crewman. This cancelled the M-21/D-21 program. A new variant of the drone, the D-21B was designed to be carried by a modified B-52H. The 4200 Test Squadron at Beale AFB received two B-52Hs (S/Ns: 61-0021 and 60-0036), which were modified to carry the D-21B. Both aircraft flew the Senior Bowl missions attempting to monitor China's nuclear weapons development in the early 1970s. All four D-21B mission were unsuccessful and the program was cancelled. This D-21 drone is one of 38 built and is on display in the Heritage Park at Beale AFB. (Both photographs by the author.)

Nine

U-2 Dragon Lady

The 99 SRS was reactivated on November 1, 1970, as a U-2C unit assigned to the 100th Strategic Reconnaissance Wing (100 SRW) operating out of U-Tapao RTAB, Thailand. The 99 SRS flew numerous missions over Southeast Asia and established a record in January 1973 with the first-ever 500 combat hours flown in a single month by a U-2 unit. By December 1974, it was flying over 600 hours a month. The 99 SRS was the last unit to leave U-Tapao RTAB when the Air Force ended operations there in 1976. SAC consolidated its high-altitude strategic reconnaissance assets in the continental United States (CONUS) under the 9 SRW at Beale AFB in 1976. The 99 SRS was assigned to the 9 SRW on June 30, 1976, giving the wing two high-altitude aircraft types on its flight line—the SR-71 and the U-2. The U-2 operations at Davis-Monthan AFB, Arizona, were transferred to Beale AFB as part of this consolidation. The first aircraft transferred was a U-2CT trainer arriving on July 12, 1976.

The 99 SRS colocated some functions with the 1 SRS and placed other functions in spaces that had previously been occupied a month prior by the B-52 unit of the 34 BS. Six U-2 hangars would eventually be built along the southeast side of the parking ramp to shelter the aircraft. The 9 SRW had three detached U-2 units: Detachment 2, Osan AB, Republic of Korea (ROK); Detachment 3, RAF Akrotiri, Cyprus; and Detachment 5, Patrick AFB, Florida.

The 17 BW that had been deactivated at Beale AFB on June 30, 1976, was reactivated as the 17th Reconnaissance Wing (17 RW) on October 1, 1982, at RAF Alconbury, United Kingdom. The 95th Reconnaissance Squadron (95 RS) was activated with the 17 RW and flew the Tactical Reconnaissance 1 (TR-1) aircraft, a close variant of the U-2R. The 17 RW and the 9 SRW would be reunited in the next war.

U-2C S/N: 56-6714 and U-2C S/N: 56-6716, 95 RS, 17 RW, RAF Alconbury, United Kingdom, are seen on the Beale AFB flight line wearing the two-tone "Sabre" grey camouflage paint scheme associated with European operations. Both aircraft were being rotated back to the CONUS from overseas service to be assigned to the 9 SRW. U-2C S/N: 56-6716 is now on display at Davis Monthan AFB, Arizona.

Capt. Edward I. Beaumont lost consciousness during a high-altitude training flight near Orville, California, while piloting U-2C S/N: 56-6714, 99 SRS, 9 SRW, on January 31, 1980. Two 9 SRW T-38 aircraft were dispatched and discovered the U-2C making a slow descending spiral. The T-38s made several close passes rocking the U-2C in an attempt to shake Captain Beaumont awake. The U-2C miraculously hit some high-tension power lines that leveled out the flight before impacting the ground. This snapped Captain Beaumont to attention before the U-2C made a belly landing in a field where he escaped with injuries. The force of the impact rendered U-2C S/N: 56-6714 inoperable and it was made into a static display at Beale AFB. This is the same aircraft shown at the top of page 92.

U-2C S/N: 56-6675, 99 SRS, 9 SRW, displays the pogo wing gears that support the wings while the U-2 is on the ground at Beale AFB. The pogos fall off upon takeoff. This aircraft was later converted to a U-2F and lost over California on February 25, 1966, when the pilot pulled up hard after an aerial refueling and the aircraft broke up in flight. The pilot ejected and survived.

Captain Gaskin returns to U-Tapao RTAB, Thailand, from a mission during the Vietnam War. Captain Gaskin and the U-2 were assigned to the 99 SRS, 100 SRW. The 99 SRS was based at this location from July 11, 1970, to June 1976. The ground crewmen have just inserted the pogos under the wings to allow the U-2 to taxi. In the background are B-52D bombers.

A U-2 flies over Beale AFB on a training flight.

A U-2 flies over the goldfields north of Beale AFB. Runway 15 can be seen in the background to the left.

This image was taken on the flight line at Beale AFB in 1974. Shown, from left to right, are Lt. Col. Stan Lawrence; Maj. Carl LaRue, standardization evaluation pilot, 95 RS, 17 SRW, RAF Alconbury, United Kingdom; TSgt. Ron Guibord; and Col. Don White, commander, 100 SRW, Beale AFB.

A TR-1A is taxiing in following a training flight at Beale AFB. The vehicle to the right is a chase car referred to as a "mobile" and is driven by a U-2/TR-1 pilot. The restricted visibility of the U-2/TR-1 during landing requires the mobile to get in behind it on the runway and call off the remaining altitude before the final touchdown.

In this image, a U-2 is about to land on Runway 15 in March 1978.

A U-2 prepares for takeoff in 1985 to support SAC's annual Exercise Global Shield.

Maintainers ride the wings of a U-2 being towed to one of the maintenance docks. This practice is done when there is little or no fuel in the U-2's wings to provide the weight to prevent the wings from bouncing and the pogo gear from coming off. In the background is a KC-135 showing why these hangars were originally referred to as nose docks.

A U-2 at Beale AFB is being marshaled into its parking spot after flying a training mission.

Ten

Desert Shield and Desert Storm

Iraq invaded Kuwait on August 2, 1990, and threatened to attack Saudi Arabia. United Nations Resolution 661 was passed calling for the restoration of Kuwaiti sovereignty on August 6. That same day, King Fahd of Saudi Arabia requested US military support to defend his country and the 9 SRW was placed on alert for deployment. The next day, the chairman of the Joint Chiefs of Staff ordered the 9 SRW to deploy two U-2s.

The first 9 SRW personnel arrived at Operating Location Crested Harvest (OL-CH), King Fahd Air Base at Taif, Saudi Arabia, on August 13. The first two 9 SRW U-2s arrived at OL-CH on August 17 and began combat operations on August 19 with Operation Olympic Flare. The 17 SRW deployed two TR-1As that arrived on August 23 and began combat operations on August 29. In all, six U-2Rs and six TR-1As were forward deployed to Saudi Arabia. This was the largest deployment of U-2s in history at that time and the first time they had been used in a tactical role. OL-CH was re-designated the 1704th Reconnaissance Squadron Provisional [1704 RS(P)] on September 21.

The Military Airlift Command's (MAC) C-5 cargo aircraft and KC-10 tankers, supplemented by the reserve commercial fleet, were having troubles meeting the demands of deploying material and personnel into theater. SAC approved the use of its KC-135 strategic tanker fleet to provide both airlift and refueling capabilities. The KC-135Qs of the 349 ARS and 350 ARS had key roles in shuttling parts, sensors, and even a U-2 engine to keep the U-2s at Taif operational.

Senior leaders in theater criticized the U-2s performance. They failed to grasp the U-2's capabilities and limitations and then placed unreasonable expectations upon it. Despite the criticism, the U-2s performed well, from saving downed F-15 crews to hunting Scud missiles. The final analysis showed the U-2s provided 10 percent of the total intelligence, over 50 percent of the imagery intelligence, and 90 percent of all US Army targeting intelligence for the entire theater.

The airmen of the 9 SRW came home to a cheering public, parades, and celebrations.

The flight line of Beale AFB is busy under an overcast sky as KC-135Q aircrews prepare to take off for Saudi Arabia in support of Operation Desert Shield. This operation was the surge of coalition forces to prevent the invasion of Saudi Arabia by Iraq.

The Beale Bandits patch was worn on the left shoulder of the KC-135Q aircrews from Beale AFB that deployed during Operation Desert Shield. The circle is light blue in black trim with a black scroll. The lettering is in gold. The image in the center shows a camel wearing a biker's helmet and leather jacket riding a KC-135Q while holding a fuel pump nozzle in his right hand.

Families and friends turned out to watch the Beale Bandits deploy. The aircrew of KC-135Q S/N: 58-0117 proudly displayed the Stars and Stripes as they prepared to taxi out. For all involved that day, there was a mixture of pride, excitement, sadness, and anxiety as the airmen of Beale AFB left loved ones behind and made the largest deployment since the Vietnam War. The KC-135s and U-2s of the 9 SRW were among the first aircraft to arrive in theater.

Five U-2Rs and TR-1As from the 99 RS, 9 SRW, Beale AFB, and the 95 RS, 17 SRW, RAF Alconbury, United Kingdom, fill a hangar at OL-CH, King Fahd Air Base at Taif, Saudi Arabia, during Operation Desert Shield/Desert Storm. The Gulf War was the largest deployment of U-2s in history. In all, six U-2Rs and six TR-1As were forward deployed to Saudi Arabia.

OL-CH was re-designated the 1704 RS(P) on September 21, 1990. The U-2s and TR-1s of the 1704 RS(P) flew 564 missions from August 19, 1990, to February 28, 1991, totaling 4,561.6 combat flying hours. The depot work, which lessened downtime traveling to and from the CONUS, was provided by 17 SRW, RAF Alconbury, United Kingdom.

The tail art on U-2R S/N: 80-1068, 9 SRW, shows a menacing green "Dragon Lady" drawn in chalk. The numbers and crosses on the tail flash are painted red. None of the aircraft were supposed to have been deployed with the 9 SRW crosses on the tail flash, but at least three have been identified with crosses on them while operating at King Fahd Air Base during the Gulf War. This aircraft had originally been the first TR-1A assigned to the 17 SRW in February 1983. It was transferred to 9 SRW in April 1987 and converted to a U-2R model.

TR-1A S/N: 80-1081, 95 RS, 17 SRW, displays a U-2 taking off with the Stars and Stripes behind it and a camel with two palm trees, representing the desert environment it is operating in.

TR-1A S/N: 80-1086, 95 RS, 17 SRW, shows a green Dragon Lady in flight.

TR-1A S/N: 80-1088, 95 RS, 17 SRW, receives a Bart Simpson in Arab dress with two palm trees design. This aircraft was lost over Orville, California, on August 7, 1996, when an onboard catastrophic failure caused it to crash into the building of the Orville newspaper *Mercury Register*. Capt. Randy Roby was killed upon ejecting. Orville resident Geraldine "Jerri" Vering was killed in the parking lot.

U-2R S/N: 80-1098 displays the black cat emblem of Detachment 2, 9 SRW, Osan AB, Republic of Korea. The original design was created by Maj. Wei-shen Chen, 35th Squadron, Republic of China Air Force (ROCAF), Taiwan. The 35th Squadron was nicknamed the "Black Cats" by the USAF personnel of Detachment H supporting the ROCAF's U-2 program. The name allegedly comes from a bar they frequented.

U-2R S/N: 68-10331, 9 SRW, displays a different variant of the Dragon Lady theme, showing a sword-wielding Asian woman with dragon wings. This aircraft was reconfigured as a U-2S in August 1996.

U-2R S/N: 68-10338, 9 SRW, displays Chester Cheetah from the Cheetos ads. This U-2 was the first to reach 20,000 hours flying time on August 11, 1994. U-2R S/N: 68-10338 was lost on August 29, 1995, when a hung pogo gear caused the aircraft to veer left upon landing and explode. Capt. David Hawkens was fatally injured upon ejecting horizontally.

TR-1A S/N: 80-1099, 95 RS, 17 SRW, displays Calvin from the famed *Calvin and Hobbes* comic strip series. Calvin, wearing goggles and holding a camera, is dressed as his "Spaceman Spiff" alter ego.

This U-2 has a shark mouth with eyes displayed on its Spur dome.

TR-1A S/N: 80-1088, 95 RS, 17 SRW, displays two different tail arts. The left flash shows the Bart Simpson at the top of page 106. The right flash shows a U-2 backed by a Dragon Lady with crossed swords, a single palm tree, and the bold letters "OL CH" across the top. The black and white photograph makes it difficult to see, but the number 88 was painted over in black and repainted in a brighter red than the original tail number color.

TR-1A S/N: 80-1070, 9 SRW, displays the Domino's Pizza Noid holding a camera in his right hand, a wand in his left, and wearing a wizard's hat. This version of Domino's Pizza Noid is commonly associated with the 1704 RS(P). Captain Lamb flew the first Senior Span mission of Desert Shield in this aircraft on August 19, 1990. TR-1A S/N: 80-1070 was reconfigured as a U-2S in February 1995.

TR-1A S/N: 80-1086, 95 RS, 17 SRW, is seen on the tarmac of King Fahd Air Base; six F-5 fighters of the Saudi Royal Air Force are in the background.

Above left is a U-2R S/N: 68-10331, 9 SRW. Above right is a U-2R S/N: 80-1068, 9 SRW. At right, a U-2R S/N: 80-1084, 9 SRW, is seen displaying a Dragon Lady's head. This aircraft was originally built as a TR-1A and delivered to the 95 RS, 17 SRW, in April 1986. It was transferred to the 9 SRW sometime between 1988 and 1989. Three F-5s of the Saudi Royal Air Force can be seen in the background.

A U-2R S/N: 68-10338, 9 SRW, is on the flight line, with an unidentified U-2 with Spur dome in the background.

U-2R S/N: 80-1076, Detachment 5, 9 SRW, of Patrick AFB, Florida, displaying the white tail art of an alligator wearing a tuxedo and top hat, was ordered painted over upon arrival at King Fahd Air Base. This aircraft was flown by Lieutenant Colonel Lloyd on the first Senior Year Electro Optical Room System (SYERS) mission on August 21, 1990, and by Maj. B.L. Bachus on the first Iraqi border crossing on January 17, 1991.

U-2R S/N: 68-10337, 9 SRW, displays a flying camel being ridden by the Black Spy from the *Spy vs. Spy* comic series in *Mad Magazine*. This aircraft was a combat veteran of the Vietnam War, flying with the 99 SRS, 100 SRW, U-Tapao RTAB, Thailand, as a U-2C.

U-2R S/N: 80-1098 is on the tarmac being prepped for a mission with a Spur dome. This aircraft was lost at Osan AB, Republic of Korea, in August 1994 when it crashed upon landing in fog. The pilot survived.

KC-135Q S/N: 59-1520 displays a white Pegasus nose art. The 9 SRW patch is above the crew hatch.

KC-135Q is seen in Saudi Arabia with its engine covers on to protect against sand. A Patriot missile battery can be seen in the background, protecting the base from Iraqi Scud missile attacks.

KC-135Q S/N: 59-1504 made a holiday delivery in December 1990 to 9 SRW airmen deployed during Operation Desert Shield. The nose art shows the Hanna-Barbera cartoon character Jabberjaw reclining on a yellow lawn chair under a gray and red umbrella. The artwork behind the 9 SRW's emblem shows Santa's sleigh pulled by three camels. The yellow banner on the sleigh contains the wing's emblem of four black crosses.

An Army passenger helps to unload KC-135Q S/N: 59-1504. The captain on the right has a Beale Bandits patch on his left shoulder that reads "Saddam Stalkers" in gold lettering on the top.

Capt. Mike Fern, wearing the patch of 749th Aerial Refueling Expeditionary Force Squadron (749 AREFS) on his right shoulder, confers with Lt. Col. Bob McCafferty.

A large "Holiday Greetings" card was sent to the men and women of the 9 SRW that were deployed during Operation Desert Shield from friends and family members back at Beale AFB. It was well received; the airmen here are looking it over to find messages from someone they know.

A first lieutenant of the 9 SRW prepares his KC-135 for takeoff. His patch indicates that he is a member of the Standardization Evaluation section of the 9th Strategic Operations Group.

Family and friends at Beale AFB await the return of the KC-135Q units deployed to Operation Desert Shield/Desert Storm.

A son sits on the shoulders of his father, waiting for his mom to return.

The first KC-135Q returning from Operation Desert Shield/Desert Storm is about to land on Runway 33 at Beale AFB and then touches down with onlookers cheering. Other KC-135Qs will be landing right behind it shortly.

Daddy is home!

Families reunite.

A member of the 9th Operational Maintenance Squadron (9 OMS) reunites with his wife.

A mother embraces her son.

A wife tearfully embraces her staff sergeant.

Eleven

THE END OF AN ERA

The huge buildup of military forces by Pres. Ronald Reagan in the 1980s succeeded in finally beating the Soviet Union in the Cold War. With the victory came the inevitable drawdown of those forces in the early 1990s. The 9 SRW was re-designated the 9th Wing on September 1, 1991. Air Force Secretary Donald Rice announced on September 17, 1991, that the Strategic Air Command (SAC), Tactical Air Command (TAC), and the Mobility Air Command (MAC) would be restructured into two new commands—Air Combat Command (ACC) and Air Mobility Command (AMC). The 9th Wing would be assigned to ACC.

Secretary of Defense Dick Cheney ordered SAC's nuclear alert forces to stand down on September 28, 1991. The Cold War was over. The 349 ARS and 350 ARS at Beale AFB were removed from alert status. SAC was finally deactivated on June 1, 1992, after 46 years of standing alert in defense of the nation. ACC was activated the same day. The 349 ARS was deactivated four days later on June 5. The 9th Wing was re-designated the 9th Reconnaissance Wing (9 RW) on October 1, 1993. The 350 ARS was assigned to AMC on that same day.

The KC-135Qs of the 350 ARS maintained their 9 SRW emblems on the right sides of their aircraft above the forward crew hatch despite the wing's re-designations and the squadron's transfer to AMC. The 350 ARS remained at Beale AFB for eight more months before transferring to McConnell AFB, Kansas.

The 350 ARS transferred to McConnell AFB, Kansas, on July 1, 1994. The sky was bright and sunny that day as the airmen of the 9 RW lined the taxiway and gave a final salute to each KC-135Q and aircrew of the 350 ARS as they taxied out to depart. The final KC-135Q roared down Runway 15 and climbed into the skies of Northern California, proudly displaying the emblem of the 9 SRW and the SAC mission it once represented. The history of Beale AFB during the Cold War came to an end with that final takeoff.

KC-135Q S/N: 58-0112, 350 ARS, 9 RW, prepares to depart Beale AFB.

Shown here is a close-up of KC-135Q S/N: 58-0112, 350 ARS, 9 RW, prior to taxiing out. The nose art shows a stegosaurus with wings refueling a pterodactyl with engines. The 9th Strategic Reconnaissance Wing emblem is above the crew hatch.

KC-135Q S/N: 58-0084, 350 ARS, 9 RW, starts to taxi out.

KC-135Q S/N: 58-0084, 350 ARS, 9 RW, receives a final salute as it taxis out.

KC-135 S/N: 59-1480, 350 ARS, 9 RW,
receives its final salute while taxiing
out. The nose art shows the cartoon
character Betty Boop dressed in a red
tuxedo jacket while sitting on a half-
moon and tipping her black top hat.

KC-135Q S/N: 58-0112, 350
ARS, 9 RW, is starting to
taxi out in this image.

KC-135Q S/N: 58-0112, 350 ARS, 9 RW, receives its final salute taxing out.

KC-135Q S/N: 58-0112 takes off for the last time down Runway 15 at Beale AFB on July 1, 1994. The KC-135Qs of the 350 ARS proudly wore the emblems of the 9th Strategic Reconnaissance Wing as they took off that day. That final symbol of Strategic Air Command at Beale AFB slowly climbed into the heavens and disappeared on the horizon as the roar of its engines faded away.

DISCOVER THOUSANDS OF LOCAL HISTORY BOOKS FEATURING MILLIONS OF VINTAGE IMAGES

Arcadia Publishing, the leading local history publisher in the United States, is committed to making history accessible and meaningful through publishing books that celebrate and preserve the heritage of America's people and places.

Find more books like this at
www.arcadiapublishing.com

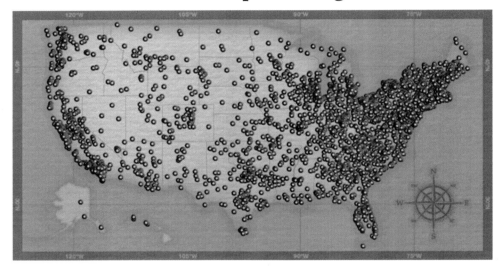

Search for your hometown history, your old stomping grounds, and even your favorite sports team.